FROM SIGHING TO SINGING

A Song For the Sighing Heart

John B. Wright

MASTER'S PRESS INC.

All biblical quotations have been taken from the King James Version unless otherwise noted.

Acknowledgments:

Song by Audrey Mieir, copyright 1959, by Manna Music, Inc., Burbank, California. Used by permission.

FROM SIGHING TO SINGING

ISBN # 0-89251-016-1
Copyright © 1976
Master's Press, Inc.

All Rights Reserved

Published by Master's Press, Inc.
20 Mills Street, Kalamazoo, MI

Printed in the United States of America

DEDICATED

To The

FIRST BAPTIST CHURCH

Little Rock, Arkansas

CONTENTS

FOREWORD

The Christian is the only person in the world who knows how to transpose sighing into singing. This is because he possesses the nature of ONE who could sigh and sing, at one and the same time. In a classic passage that describes our Saviour's passion, Isaiah places side by side the *sorrow* and the *satisfaction* of Jehovah's Servant: "He is . . . 'the' man of sorrows. . . . He . . . shall be satisfied" (Isaiah 53:3, 11). The writer to the Hebrews includes the joy and the cross in one sentence: "Looking unto Jesus the author and finisher of our faith; who for the *joy* that was set before him endured the *cross*, despising the shame, and is set down at the right hand of the throne of God"

(Hebrews 12:2). To know this "faith of the Son of God" is to be able to say with the apostle Paul: "As sorrowful, yet always rejoicing" (II Corinthians 6:10).

In a world of chaos and crying we must know afresh the secret of transposing sighing into singing; and so I welcome and commend Dr. John B. Wright's little book on this subject. I am happy to do this because these sermons are biblical expositions with practical applications. Writing as a pastor of a large congregation, my friend, John Wright, does not offer a human panacea but rather shares the divine provision for victorious living. It is my prayer that God will richly bless a needed message in a needy hour.

Stephen F. Olford
Minister-at-Large
Encounter Ministries, Inc.
Holmes Beach, Florida

INTRODUCTION

Psalm 137 is a song of bitter lament composed during or immediately after the Babylonian Exile of God's chosen people. They were captives in a strange land. The recollection of their own country and the holy temple where they had sung glad songs of praise to their God caused bitter weeping. It was a time for sadness and sighing, not mirth and singing. Their Babylonian captors jeeringly called for songs of Zion, but the children of Israel could not respond; their hearts were overwhelmed with grief. So it is with the Christian when sin and unbelief have made him captive; he or she cannot sing the Lord's song in a strange land. The joy and victorious singing of the Christ-like life gives way to depression and a defeated sighing.

Sighing and singing represent the two life styles available to every believer. One of the reasons for the lamentable lack of achievement of the average Christian is that he has adopted the life style of sighing defeat in preference to that of singing victory. Christianity to him is routine, not romance.

A shipping firm competing with the air lines for overseas passengers advertised that travel to Europe by boat would take several days, but one would enjoy the luxury of games, recreation, leisure time, and evening entertainment. Admittedly, reaching the desired destination would require more time, but the firm's argument was supported by the striking conclusion that "Getting there is half the fun."

Through faith in Christ many professing Christians have set out for the destination that we all know as heaven. They believe that heaven is a place of peace, joy, and rest. Struggling through life with a series of sighs they are saying, in effect, "If I can just make it to heaven I'll be all right, for then there will be singing!" Their concept of heaven is true enough but they fail to realize it really is true that "Getting there is half the fun!"

Heaven beyond the grave is a continuation of blessings entered THIS side of the grave. The attitude of sighing on this side and singing on the other side contradicts what the Scriptures teach about life in Christ. The purpose of this book is to inspire the Christian who has "hung his harp upon the willows" to once again sing the Lord's song.

We will examine the causes underlying this attitude of defeat and resources available to every believer, hoping to enable him or her to live the victorious life in Christ. This does not imply, of course, that all the Christian's problems will immediately melt away, or that Satan cannot tempt a victorious Christian, or that God will not chasten His disobedient children. But it will give the assurance that the problems are not insurmountable, and that there CAN be real joy and peace. The temptations of Satan can be faced with confidence that God has given us *"the victory through our Lord Jesus Christ"* (1 Corinthians 15:57). There can be a real eagerness to do the will of the Father and to accept His loving discipline.

Many, indeed most, Christians experience feelings of inadequacy, defeat, and depression at one time or another. Too often these feelings are allowed to control us. We become "sighing" Christians. We become resigned to a life of struggle and defeat because we fail to see both the purpose and provision of God. You do not have to respond to trials and unexpected difficulties by being resigned to your fate. The Christian must have his attention focused on Christ and not on his daily struggles, or on himself.

From sighing defeat to singing victory is one of life's most exciting transitions. This book is written with the prayer that upon reading it you will experience such a transition in YOUR life.

PART I

THE REALITY OF SIGHING

ITS INESCAPABLENESS

Psalm 11

Trials are common to man. You are either in a trial, coming out of a trial, or going into a trial. Since none of us is exempt from trials we need to learn how to respond to them.

Our first reaction may be to attempt to escape, only to learn that, for a time at least, the present crisis is inescapable. The easiest thing to do is to concede defeat and flee. In the 11th Psalm David faced an apparently overwhelming problem. His friends admonished him to "flee to the mountain." With confidence that God would deliver him, he retorted, *"Why say ye to my soul, flee as a bird to the mountain?"* (v. 1). If anyone had justifiable reasons to flee, David certainly did.

He suffered not only from those who hated him but also from those whom he trusted. We sometimes suffer at the hands of our enemies, but the most severe pain can be inflicted by misguided friends. David was asked, *"If the foundations be destroyed, what can a just man do?"* (v. 3). Some of you this very moment feel sure foundations crumbling beneath you, threatening the one thing in life you hold dear. A dark cloud hangs ominously over your head. You stand desperately in need of a friend who has an encouraging word, only to have that friend say to you as David's friends said to him,

"There is nothing you can do. Your case is hopeless." Yet you know better.

David's foes were unrelenting in their determination to defeat him. He described their clandestine method of attack in verse 2, *"For lo the wicked bend their bow. They make ready their arrow upon the string that they may privily shoot at the upright in heart."* These foes had their arrows aimed, and positioned in a secret place on a moonlit night. All of us are exposed to the furtive behavior of a foe who is sneaky in his approach. We never know when his bow is bent, his arrow aimed in our direction. We are vulnerable to such attacks and must expect their sudden onslaught.

When faced with this inescapable trial David could have responded with sighing or singing. He chose to sing. David was able to sing because he knew the power of God, the perception of God, the passion of God, and the punishment of God. An understanding of these four things can change YOUR sighing into singing.

"The Lord is in his holy temple, the Lord's throne is in heaven: his eyes behold, his eyelids try, the children of men" (v. 4). The Lord is still upon the throne. He has not lost control of the universe He has created. He has not abdicated that throne or deserted His responsibility. He is the omnipotent God of the universe and nothing comes to Him by surprise. Nothing happens to us without first of all receiving His permission.

There is no sorrow or trial in life for which God

is not adequate. The story is told of a South African who paid $35,000 for a Rolls Royce automobile and demanded to know the engine's horsepower. The dealer informed him that the manufacturer would not allow such information to be divulged. The customer's remonstrance was so severe, the dealer wired London requesting information about the engine's horsepower. The manufacturer replied with one word, "Adequate." Regardless of the severity of your trial, the Lord is supremely adequate to turn your sighing into singing.

The Lord does not always deliver one FROM the circumstance, but He invariably delivers IN the circumstance. The experience of Daniel and the three Hebrew children illustrates this truth. These young men were keenly aware of God's presence. We may say, "I wish I could feel God's presence near me like that." Our problem is that we want it outside the den and outside the furnace.

In Ezekiel's vision he was led into a river in the desert and the waters were risen so that he could not pass over. The prophet's triumphant note was sounded as he pealed forth "...*and he brought me through*" (Ezekiel 47:1-6). The Lord always brings us through.

> Some through the waters, some through the flood,
> Some through the fire, but all through the blood;
> Some through great sorrow, but God gives a song
> In the night season and all the day long.

THE PERCEPTION OF GOD

"The Lord is in his holy temple, the Lord's throne is in heaven: his eyes behold, his eyelids try, the children of men" (v. 4). God is not far away. He is not removed from the fray. He is in the middle of the arena. His eyes behold. All this simply means that God sees the trial and is aware of the conflict.

Our trials have a way of blinding us so that we cannot see all that He sees in the way of reinforcements. A classic example of this truth comes from the life of Elisha as he was surrounded by the horses and chariots of the king of Syria (2 Kings 6:8-17). The prophet's servant rose early and beheld the host that compassed the city and said to Elisha, *"Alas! my master; how shall we do?"* This piercing question is one that has fallen from many querulous lips: "Alas! what shall we do?" The prophet answered, *"Fear not: for they that be with us are more than they that be with them. And Elisha prayed and said, 'Lord, I pray thee, open his eyes, that he may see.' And the Lord opened the eyes of the young man; and he saw: and, behold, the mountain was full of horses and chariots of fire round about Elisha."* God whose "eyes behold" sees the reinforcements ready to be supplied at the signal. As a boy I remember frequently singing an old song of these re-inforcements:

Ho, my comrades! see the signal
Waving in the sky!
Reinforcements now appearing,

Victory is nigh

Chorus

"Hold the fort, for I am coming,"
Jesus signals still;
Wave the answer back to heaven,
"By Thy grace we will."

See the mighty host advancing,
Satan leading on;
Mighty men around us falling,
Courage almost gone!
See the glorious banner waving!
Hear the trumpet blow!
In our Leader's name we triumph
Over every foe.

Fierce and long the battle rages,
But our help is near;
Onward comes our great Commander,
Cheer, my comrades, cheer!
The reinforcement is the watchful and com-
passionate gaze of our Commander, the Lord
Jesus Christ.

THE PASSION OF GOD

*"The Lord trieth the righteous: but the wicked and him
who loveth violence his soul hateth"* (v. 5). Not only
does God sit on His throne and observe through
watchful eye the conflict: He puts His feeling into

it. The passion of our Lord is revealed in His love for us.

The words "the Lord trieth the righteous" reveal His love for us. Periods of testing are to be interpreted as expressions of love because the Lord is preparing us for bigger and perhaps more difficult things. The fact that trials and testings come to you is a sign that the Lord loves you. I can see in my own life how God has arranged for lesser trials to test me and condition me for the greater ones. The Lord is good to prepare us through testings for the severe conflicts in life. Jeremiah said, *"If thou hast run with the footmen, and they have wearied thee, then how canst thou contend with horses? and if in the land of peace wherein thou trustedst, they wearied thee, then how wilt thou do in the swelling of Jordan?"* (Jeremiah 12:5). We will certainly do poorly facing major crises in our life if we have wearied in facing the minor ones.

THE PUNISHMENT OF GOD

"Upon the wicked he shall rain snares, fire and brimstone, and an horrible tempest: this shall be the portion of their cup" (v. 6). We should never allow the conflict to sap us of our energy and time to the extent that we lose consciousness of the One who is commanding the battle. He will command the battle and face the trial in His power. We have one responsibility in the conflict, and that is to praise the Lord who is in command. Years ago I heard the story of a little girl who was saved, and the pastor inquired, "Where is Jesus now?" She replied, "In

my heart." The pastor then asked, "What are you going to do when Satan knocks at your door?" The little girl answered, "I'm going to just sit still and ask Jesus to answer the door. Then Jesus will come back and say, 'We defeated him, didn't we?' " "But why do you say 'we'?" her pastor asked. "For Jesus will reply, 'You did the sitting and I did the answering.' " That is the way we should face all our problems. When the devil sees Jesus at the door he recognizes the One who defeated him at Calvary, and moves on. The key to meeting every crisis is a willingness to depend on God. This dependency is evident in Jehoshaphat's battle with the Ammonites and the Moabites in 2 Chonicles 20:15. God said, *"...For the battle is not yours, but God's...ye shall not need to fight this battle; set yourselves, stand still and see the salvation of the Lord."* Later in the chapter we read *"...and when they began to sing and to praise, the Lord set ambushments against the children of Ammon, Moab, and Mount Seir, which were come against Judah; and they were smitten"* (vs. 22).

It is an impressive picture of Jehoshaphat and his men entering the battle singing the praises of God amid the clash of swords and the shout of war. This unusual behavior so frustrated the enemy that they turned on themselves and destroyed one another. When Jehoshaphat returned from the battlefield it was covered with the bodies of his fallen opponents, but he had not even unsheathed his sword. This is the way Christian warfare and daily conflicts should be faced. It is a sad day when the Christian exchanges his hymnbook for a sword and enters the conflict, regardless of what that conflict may be. God loves us, and His hatred for anything that threatens us will cause Him to enter the battle and defeat the foe. We must not forget the principle of dependency.

A preacher recalled that his mother would come to him during a quarrel with his brother and say, "If you can't sing it, don't say it." The Christian faith was begotten on the wings of song and should be lived out in song. Are you surrounded by threats that seem inescapable? Would you like to flee? You must not retreat from the battle. But remember there is a person to whom you can flee.

Flee as a bird to your mountain, Thou who art
    weary of sin;
Go to the clear, flowing fountain, Where you
    may wash and be clean;
Fly, for th' Avenger is near thee; Call, and the
    Savior will hear thee;
O thou who art weary of sin.

He is the bountiful Giver, Now unto Him
    draw near;
Peace then shall flow like a river, Thou shalt
    be saved from thy fear.
Hark! 'tis the Savior calling! Haste! for the twi-
    light is falling!
Flee, for the night is appalling! And thou shalt

be saved from thy fear,
And thou shalt be saved from thy fear.

He will protect thee forever, Wipe every falling
tear;
He will forsake thee, no, never, Sheltered so
tenderly there.
Haste, then the hours are flying, Spend not the
moments in sighing,
Cease from your sorrow and crying; The Savior
will wipe every tear.
The Savior will wipe every tear.

Come, then, to Jesus, they Savior, He will redeem
thee from sin;
Blest with a sense of His favor, Make thee all
glorious within!
Call, for the Savior is near thee, Waiting in mercy
to hear thee;
He by His presence will cheer thee, O thou who
art weary of sin,
O thou who art weary of sin.

ITS BITTERNESS

Psalm 12

Trials are never pleasant; often they are bitter.
We soon learn, however, that the sweets of life
are found in the places of former conflict. As Samson journeyed to Timnath, a young lion roared out
against him. The Spirit of the Lord came upon him,
and he rent the lion as he would have rent a kid.
Retracing his steps days later, he turned aside and
found a swarm of bees and honey in the carcass
of the lion. Scripture says, *"He took thereof in his
hands, and went on, eating"* (Judges 13:5-9). The scene
of your bitter conflict may also be the scene of your
greatest blessing.

In Psalm 12 we see once again David's experience
of a bitter trial, but out of the trial came a
blessed promise.

THE BITTER TRIAL

*"Help Lord: for the godly man ceaseth; for the faith-
ful fail from among the children of men"* (v. 1). David
voiced the bitterness of his persecution at the hands
of a GODLESS CHARACTER. He saw all around him
evidence that the faithful are few; disloyalty, self-
centeredness, and deception are the norm. The
world is full of unprincipled people who are guided
not by what is right, but by what is expedient. If
it will insure personal gain, an unprincipled person

will engage in the most unethical and unscrupulous practice, knowing others will suffer by it. One of David's bitter experiences was to fall victim to such an ungodly character. In desperation he cried out to God for help. You, too, may fall victim to someone who has no moral scruples. Perhaps you have already been hurt by someone who wronged you, and you can testify to the bitterness of the experience.

Next, there is the trial of WORTHLESS COMMITMENTS. "For the faithful fail from among the children of men." The word "faithful" suggests commitment, and in David's experience many had failed in this commitment. It seems today that people find it difficult to really commit themselves to anything and stay with it. Many marriages are entered into with the idea that if it doesn't work, the partners can give it up as a bad deal and go their separate ways. Perhaps you are the victim of a broken marriage because your partner's commitment was worthless, and you are experiencing the bitterness of such failure. It could be you are suffering because of your own worthless commitment due to your capriciousness and unwillingness to stay where the going is tough until a goal is achieved. I have often said if I took one step every time I wanted to resign, I would be in the middle of the Pacific Ocean. When such a temptation floods my soul, I always respond with the words of the poet:

I want to let go, but I won't let go;

There are battles to fight, by day and by night;
And for God and the right, and I won't let go.
I want to let go, but I won't let go;
What? Lie down on the field, and surrender
   my shield?
No. I will not let go.
I want to let go, but I won't let go;
I am sick, it is true, worried and blue;
And worn through and through, but I won't let go.
I want to let go, but I won't let go;
May this be my song through legions of wrong;
O, God, keep me strong that I may never let go.

Another of David's bitter trials was that of CARELESS CONVERSATION. In verse 2 he said, *"They speak vanity every one with his neighbor: with flattering lips and with a double heart do they speak."* David's own commitment, integrity, and godliness were tried through a godless character, a worthless commitment, and a careless conversation. You, perhaps, can speak personally of the bitter trial of careless conversations that have been hurtful to you, if not injurious to your character. The unwholesome conversation that David referred to was expressed in three ways.

Their conversation was flippant: *"They speak vanity."* I once thought that when the Bible spoke of idle talk it meant profanity or smutty stories. But now I am convinced that idle talk is any conversation that doesn't glorify Christ. If the average conversation were shorn of its frivolity, precious little would be said. If you want to discover how injurious idle talk can be, examine closely the barbs made in jest toward one another. Underneath the humorous barb, generally, is an intention to tell that person what we really think without appearing to do so. Many persons have gone home from a party or a get-together of some kind and reflected upon such a barb, wondering what was actually intended by it. Sometimes we robe an honest remark in a garment of humor and flippancy, and the result is always painful. The frivolous tongue is a sharp instrument: the wounds it inflicts penetrate deep into the soul.

Their conversation was full of flattery: *"with flattering lips...do they speak."* If the Body life of the church is healthy and functioning properly, the members will have an openness that will enable them to share mutual weaknesses with one another. But the contrary is too often true. Have you ever listened to a sermon that didn't speak to you, but in leaving the church you expressed pleasure to the pastor? To compliment or flatter in an insincere way is to do injury to the one being complimented.

Their conversation was full of falsehood: *"...with a double heart do they speak."* David could have said "with a forked tongue they speak." James tells us that sweet and bitter water do not come from the same spring (James 3:9-11), and the double-minded man is unstable in all his ways (1:8). When I was a boy, we would have said of such a person, "He is anybody's dog who will hunt with him." This kind of person alters his conversation depending on the audience.

THE BURDENED PRAYER

In view of the bitter trial, David was convinced that nothing short of an immediate and powerful intervention of God would meet the crisis. Thus he talked to God, and through burdened prayer made a threefold appeal for deliverance.

He prayed for deliverance from those having an UNHOLY PRIDE: *"The Lord shall cut off all flattering lips, and the tongue that speaketh proud things"* (v. 3). It is usually unholy pride that causes one to defame a brother through careless conversation. The proud person will attempt to exalt himself by discrediting another. Therefore, David prayed for protection from their unholy pride. He asked God to protect him from their unholy persistence: *"Who have said, With our tongue will we prevail; our lips are our own: who is Lord over us?"* (v. 4). Persistence can be a virtue, but in this case it is a tenacious refusal to yield to God. No tool is used by Satan more effectively in inflicting injury than a persistent tongue spreading gossip. Paul said of such people, *"...they learn to be idle, wandering about from house to house; and not only idle but tattlers also, and busybodies, speaking things which they ought not"* (1 Timothy 5:13). Proverbs 18:8 says, *"The words of a talebearer are as wounds and they go down into the innermost parts of the belly."*

Finally, David prayed for deliverance from their

UNHOLY POSSESSION "...*our lips are our own...*" His antagonists were insisting that no one, including God, was going to tell them how to use their lips. "These are our own lips," they cried, "and who is Lord over us?" An unholy use of the tongue results when the offender fails to acknowledge the lordship of Christ, which includes the mastery over our speech.

THE BLESSED PROMISE

Just as Samson found honey in the carcass of the lion, so we can expect promise to be found in the midst of our bitter trials. This blessed promise can be described in four ways.

It can be understood in its ELOCUTION. *For the oppression of the poor, for the sighing of the needy, now will I arise, saith the Lord; I will set him in safety from him that puffeth at him* (v. 5). Elocution, the art of speaking, refers to the eloquence with which one speaks. The text says, concerning the promise, *"saith the Lord."* It is a promise given us directly from the Lord, and He has never broken any promise which He has given. The promise does not come to us hearsay. It is not a rumor. It is not what we have heard from the lips of man. God has spoken it Himself.

Next, there is the EXECUTION of the promise. God says, "I will arise." Not only does God speak a promise; He will arise and execute that promise. The Bible speaks of God sitting upon His throne. He is looking down from heaven, observing our conflict, and He arises from His throne and enters the contest. He does not sit passively by and watch His own children being battered and buffeted by the devil; He graciously gives us the strength to overcome such "fiery darts" (Ephesians 6:16).

Following the execution of the promise is the EXPLANATION of the promise. Verse 5 is a wonderful statement of assurance: *"For the oppression of the poor, the sighing of the needy, now will I arise saith the Lord: I will set him in safety from him that puffeth at him."* The word "puffeth" describes those who would ensnare David. The believer will always have something that puffs at him. What or who is puffing at you? Is it your job? your companion? a problem in the church? turbulence in the home? Is something at this moment holding you captive? Are you ensnared by some tyrant who puffs at you? This promise is for YOU. God explains the promise and reminds you that it is for YOU, and He will set you free.

Finally, we have the ELEVATION of the promise: *"The words of the Lord are pure words: as silver tried in a furnace of the earth, purified seven times"* (vs. 6).

The promises of human beings are fallible and unreliable. The speech of man is marked by impurities. The antithesis to the promises of mortal man are the promises of the eternal God whose words are like those made pure, tried in the furnace of the earth. Faithful are the promises of God, for they are elevated far and beyond those of man (Isaiah 53:8,9).

How wonderful it is to know that the words uttered by our Lord to His children transcend any human expression! Every word is free of emptiness and superficiality, with no trace of sham or affectation in His promises. We join with all the saints of all the ages and loudly exclaim: "He has never broken any promise; He will keep His promise to me!"

We, like the Apostle Paul, are fully persuaded that what He has promised He is able also to perform (1 Thessalonians 4:34).

Hallelujah! What a Savior!

ITS DURABLENESS

Psalm 13

The Psalmist said: *"Tears may endure for the night, but joy cometh in the morning"* (Psalm 30:15). But you say, "That certainly is not the case with me. My tears have not been transient, but have settled down and made themselves at home in my heart. They are my constant companions."

We have been thinking of David's trials and his prayer for deliverance. In the 13th Psalm he expressed a fear that his trials would abide with him forever. He cried out in desperation, "How long? How long?" Four times in this brief psalm he made that plaintive cry. It seems that when we have a discordant string we play it more than all the others. He repeated, "How long...how long?" You may be bombarded by trials this very moment, and you find yourself sighing with David, how long, how long? There is good news for you in this psalm, for it speaks of the durability of sighing, the demands in sighing, and the delight through sighing.

THE DURABILITY OF THE SIGHING

The sighing in David's life endured as long as he harbored certain attitudes toward God, attitudes that were unwholesome. Sighing is usually a symptom of a deeper root-problem rather than simply the problem itself. The underlying problem is most often a wrong attitude toward God. The life style of the Israelites during their wilderness wandering was one of sighs and groans. Moses became weary of their murmurings and entreated the Lord for deliverance from their complaints. Moses was assured that it was not he at whom they were angry, but God. It became evident that the reason for their sighing was a wrong attitude toward God.

In my years in the pastorate I have experienced the lashing of people who reacted to the truth expounded from God's word. I used to take that personally until I learned it was not I with whom they were angry, but God. It is humorous, yet pathetic, the number of people in any given instance who will accuse the minister of preaching directly to them. It is the sense of guilt which is a result of an estranged relationship with God that usually produces such feelings. Such people are known for their sighing, but never for their singing. They are always unhappy. David gave us the key to this habitual sighing in verse 1 where he expressed an unrighteous attitude toward God. He accused God of being forgetful. *"How long wilt thou forget me, O Lord? for ever?"* Have you ever been so baffled by the problems of life, so puzzled by its perplexities that you thought God had forgotten you? But God does not forget. It has been said that God has a "Book for our thoughts" (Malachi 3:16), a "Bag for our transgressions" (Job 14:17), and a "Bottle for our tears" (Psalm 41:8). This imagery clearly shows that our tears are precious to Him, and He is ever aware when they are shed. To be surrounded by friends who share our sorrow is comforting, but to know that no tear shed in secret falls without our Lord's notice is a thought to be treasured. His promise *"Lo, I am with you always"* has no limitations.

Alexander McClaren has been a favorite expositor of mine through the years. When he was sixteen he accepted his first job in Glasgow, sixteen miles from home. He and his father had a relationship that any father and son would covet. Since this was the first time Alexander would be away from home, his father insisted he return Saturday night. Remembering the deep ravine between home and Glasgow, and the terrible things that were supposed to have happened in its inky darkness, Alexander suggested that he return Sunday morning. His father said, "No, Alex, Saturday night. I will be so anxious to see you." Saturday night came, and with fear and trembling Alexander approached the dreaded ravine. Forcing himself to continue the journey into its blackness he heard the sounds of someone approaching, and as he turned to run, he recognized that the man emerging from the ravine was his father. Although his father knew he was scared to death, he only said, "Alex, I have missed you so badly I could not wait to see you, and wanted to come to meet you." Into the ravine they walked arm in arm, and the haunted abyss held no terror.

Are you sighing today because you feel God has forgotten you? He has not abandoned you. He is now present if you will but open the eyes of your understanding.

David's sighing attitude lingered because of his mistaken impression that God was UNKIND. He inquired of the Lord, *"how long wilt thou hide thy face from me?"* (vs. 1). To turn one's face from a needy person would be an impolite and unkind gesture. David was accusing God of such unkindness. In Scripture the Holy Spirit is symbolized by the dove (Matthew 3:16). Among many outstanding qualities of the dove is its loving nature, as portrayed beautifully in the Song of Solomon. When the dove comes to a stream to drink he never cranes his neck or looks up, but keeps his eye on the water, just as we fasten our eyes on the object of our devotion. The delight of our Lord is His beloved, and as the dove fastens its eyes upon the stream, our Lord's eyes are upon us. If you are sighing today it could be that you have forgotten that God delights in you. He has not turned His back on you. Isaiah 62:4 reminds us, *"for the Lord delighteth in thee."*

Finally David's state of despondency came from his supposition that God had neglected him. He cried, *"How long?...How long?"* David felt that God was not only forgetful and unkind, but also neglectful. He repeated this lament four times in six verses, indicating that he had developed a life style of sighing. Our conversation becomes more negative than positive when we lapse into such a life style. You never inquire about the health of some people because their response is too time-consuming. Their cry is, "How long? How long?" Such a person each morning looks out the window and says, "Oh, my, it's worse today."

THE DESIRES IN THE SIGHING

David's despondent sighing finally caused him to cry out to God in prayer. When life is placid and free of trouble we have a tendency to neglect our prayer life, but when sighing overwhelms us we turn our eyes upward. David prayed that he would be granted peace. This should be the desire of every sighing heart.

First, he expressed a desire for the PEACE OF CONSIDERATION. *"Consider and hear me,"* he prayed (vs. 3). We all want consideration. My ambition as a young boy in junior high school was to be considered for the basketball team. I did not qualify. As a high school freshman, I tried out for the bass horn, but my best friend was chosen over me. I was not accepted. In my first year of college I was considered for the men's quartet, but once again was rejected. At the age of eighteen I began to sense that God was calling me into the ministry. I was so defeated by the inferiority complex that characterized my life, so haunted by my past experience of never being chosen to do anything important, that this possibility of service was overwhelming. I could hardly believe that God would consider me for His Kingdom work. I did not just surrender to the call; I jumped at the chance. My astonishment of His continual consideration of me is unabated after these twenty-seven years.

Psalm 16:6 describes accurately God's dealing with me. The Psalmist said, speaking of the goodness of God, *"The lines are fallen unto me in pleasant places."* The lines spoken of here refer to the measuring line marking off an estate to which one has fallen heir. When God revealed to me in those early years that He was considering me, my mind could not comprehend the pleasant places He was to mark out by His line. It seems that He has given me His finest churches, and no more "pleasant places" could be found in all the earth. Oh, the joy, the inexpressible joy of being the object of His loving consideration!

If you are despairing and sighing, thinking no one cares, I want to tell you God cares. You matter to Him and are considered by Him. Think of the peace that comes from knowing that God does have consideration for you.

Continuing to cry out to God, David desired the PEACE OF ILLUMINATION. He prayed, *"lighten mine eyes, lest I sleep the sleep of death"* (vs. 3). Two options are open to every believer in danger of being blinded by Satan. One is to pray for illumination; the other is to settle down into a kind of death. Satan can so blind us that we become insensitive to the promptings of the Holy Spirit.

It is sad to see how effective Satan is in blinding the eyes of men, causing them to commit the most ignominious acts. A young lady came to me

recently who had been present in one of our serv-
ices the week before. My sermon was on the im-
morality of the church in Corinth, and the Holy
Spirit convicted her of a life style of prodigality.
She came to tell me that upon returning to her
apartment she ordered the man out of the house
with whom she had been living. The Holy Spirit
illumined her eyes, and she saw for the first time
blindness producing moral death. Such blindness
always leads to a dead end.

When our youngest daughter, Patty, was in the
first grade, her teacher informed us of her inability
to see clearly distinguished figures on the black-
board. We immediately made an appointment with
an eye doctor, and he astonished us by saying she
should have had glasses when she was two years
of age. After the glasses were fitted, I asked if she
should be required to wear them constantly. He
replied, "Once she sees she will never want to be
without them." Upon putting the glasses on, she lit-
erally stared at the trees and the lawn. For a moment I did not realize that she was seeing individual
leaves and blades of grass for the first time. Prior
to having the new lens she saw the world as a
"glob" and thought God had made it that way,
for as far as she knew, her vision was normal.
The physician was right. She is never without her
glasses. She had thought her vision was normal
and missed many beautiful things as a result. Many
Christians in our churches are blinded to the exciting things available through life in Christ, and have

settled down to a mediocre existence thinking this is normal Christianity. Do you desire something better? It is available. Pray that God will enlighten your eyes that you may be awakened from your spiritual slumber.

Finally, David asked for PEACE OF PROTECTION. He prayed, *"Lest mine enemy say, I have prevailed against him"* (vs. 4). He wanted to be pacified with the confidence of protection. He did not want the enemy ever to say, "I have conquered him."

You and I need never fear danger. Years ago a missionary to China, Marie Munson, was on board a ship that was captured by pirates. One pirate, with the intention of assaulting her, came into her cabin and pointed a revolver at her face. She said quietly, "The Lord will not let you pull that trigger, for He said, *'No weapon that is formed against thee shall prosper.'* " The pirate turned and left, and the missionary went to bed and slept soundly through the night. She experienced the peace of God's protection. We all come under this protection. Why fear?

THE DELIGHT FROM THE SIGHING

The delight in deliverance from sighing is seen in verse 6 where David burst forth with the loud assertion, *"I will sing unto the Lord, because he hath dealth bountifully with me."* From sighing to singing is a delight we all can enjoy. You may be asking, "How can I be delivered from this sighing and experience the delight of song?" Two aspects of this delight are mentioned in the 13th Psalm.

It is important to understand how David attained joy through his trials. It is helpful to recall the past faithfulness of God to us. David said, *"But I have trusted in thy mercy"* (verse 5). He recollected times when he trusted in the mercy of God. If your life style is one of sighing, think back over the past years when you trusted God and He brought you through. By remembering God's unchanging faithfulness in past difficulties, you will be encouraged to trust Him in the present crisis. This text can free you from your habitual sighing and enable you to enjoy your Christian life.

"Singing I go along my way, praising the Lord,
  praising the Lord,
 Singing I go along my way, for Jesus has
  taken my load."

The Christian who wants to face trials and difficulties with joy and thanksgiving rather than with despair and sighing must make a deliberate effort to break away from old patterns of thinking and acting. David resolved, *"my heart shall rejoice in thy salvation"* (vs. 5).

When our son left for college to prepare for the ministry, I wanted to give him a parting word he would remember. I said, "Phillip, it isn't desire that determines your destiny: it is discipline." Now let me say to you, if you are in a spiritual muddle and your life is a series of sighs, you won't pray your way out; you won't read your way out; you won't wait your way out; you won't find your way out by going to conferences. By a definite act of your will, through self-discipline, you will deliberately walk out of it. A small boy dressed in white shirt and tie walked with his mother to church one Sunday morning, following a rain. A mud puddle proved to be a challenge to him, and he attempted to jump to the other side, only to land right in the middle. The exasperated mother said to the obstreperous lad, "John, what ARE you going to do next?" He replied confidently "I'm going to get up." This is exactly the resolution you must make. Any other decision will leave you in the mud puddle of sighing.

If you have been delivered from an attitude of habitual sighing to one of delight in all that God is, you will show it. There will be unmistakable evidence of the transformation from sighing defeat to singing victory. You can say with David, *"I will sing unto the Lord"* (vs. 6). While in London recently, my wife and I visited Buckingham Palace. Our guide informed us that when the flag was up over the palace it indicated the Queen was in residence. That day she was not, and we were disappointed. Joy is the flag that flies over the soul, signifying the King is in residence. If you have been delivered from sighing, others will know of your delight by the joy on your face.

The deliberate reflection on who God is and what He has done for you will free you from continually sighing over your problems. God has

done wonderful things for you.
It makes good sense to sing!

PART II

THE REASON FOR SIGHING

BLIND TO THE PURPOSE OF GOD

Romans 8:28

Our sighing, for the most part, is the result of our discontent over certain circumstances that presently surround us. Too often our happiness depends upon what happens to us. Someone has said, "If our happenings happen to happen happily we have happiness. If our happenings happen to happen unhappily we have unhappiness." One's satisfaction and happiness should not depend on one's circumstances, but rather on one's relationship with Christ.

Second Corinthians 2:14 records what Paul said our response to every circumstance should be: *"Now thanks be unto God, which always causeth us to triumph in Christ, and maketh manifest the savour of his knowledge by us in every place."* Notice he says we triumph "always in every place." There is no circumstance not included here. "Always" refers to time; "in every place" refers to location. This includes every kind of circumstance you will ever face, and Paul said you can triumph over it. There is no excuse for a Christian ever to sigh instead of sing. One of the secrets to a life of singing, as we shall see in this chapter, is understanding that God has a purpose in every trial. This truth is clearly taught in the familiar twenty-eighth verse of Romans 8: *"And we know that all things*

*work together for good to them that love God, to them
who are the called according to his purpose.* "Blindness
to the truth that God works "all things together for
our good" usually leads to a life of habitual sighing.

The sweep of the statement "all things" is all-
inclusive. All things—both animate and inanimate
—are included. This chapter will reveal how "these
things" act in a way so as to serve our good. There
are four ways in which "these things" act.

ALL THINGS ACT VIGOROUSLY

The fact that the whole creation is busily engaged, working in your behalf, making everything
to serve your good, should cause you to sing the
Lord's song even though you are in a strange land
(Psalm 137:3-4). Everything is working for our
good, although everything in itself is not good.

Notice first the PURPOSE OF THE WORK. If all of
God's creation is working energetically and aggres-
sively there must be a purpose. The purpose is to
bring to fruition God's plan and His will for the
life of every believer. His plan is that we be conformed into the image of His Son (Romans
12:1; 8:29).

In years past a workman would stand over his
smeltering pot where the ore was being melted by
the tremendous heat. As the impurities rose to the
surface, the worker would skim them off. He would
know all the impurities were removed when he
could bend over the pot and see a reflection of
his face in the pure metal. With his work fin-

ished for the day he would stoop, turn out the fire, and go home.

Today you may feel you are in the fire, and the pain is unbearable. God is more concerned in changing you than He is in changing your circumstances. Romans 8:28 cannot be understood apart from verse 29: *"For whom he did foreknow, he also did predestinate to be conformed to the image of His Son . . . ."* He keeps us in the fire until He, like the workman, sees the image of His face.

Next we see the PROPULSION OF THE WORK. To form sinful creatures into the image of our Lord requires a source of power that transcends all human effort and skill. The propulsion for this work is God and God alone. A beautiful illustration of this truth comes from an architectural phenomenon in Spain. Outside Madrid stands the famed Escorial ancient monastery of the Augustinians, the order to which Martin Luther belonged. The kings of Spain have been buried there for centuries. The church is a magnificent example of stately beauty. The architect who designed the building made an arch that was so flat, it frightened the king, who ordered the architect to add a column that would uphold the middle of the arch. The architect remonstrated that it was not necessary, but the king insisted. The column was built. Years later, after the king died, the architect revealed that the column was a quarter of an inch shorter than the arch; but the arch had never sagged in the slightest. Today the guides have a method of passing a lath between the column and the arch which has stood through the centuries as mute proof of the rightness of the architect's knowledge. The plan of God needs no human arguments, no human column required to buttress it. People build their little columns, but God has a way of making them fall a bit short so that in the end it can always be demonstrated that His plan, like the arch, rests on its own foundation and needs no other support. God's plan precludes all human effort. At times we may think God's plan has a flaw in it. We attempt to support it by our buttresses or react against it, not realizing that it is all a part of God's plan, and to tamper with it is sin.

Next, there is the PERPETUITY OF THE WORK. God will continue with infinite patience to conform us into the image of His Son regardless of how many times we are marred by a stubborn resistance or willful sin. He is the embodiment of love; and love, Paul said, *"suffereth long"* (1 Corinthians 13:4).

Such love was demonstrated in the life of a young nurse who astonished her friends by appearing at church one Sunday morning with her face a mass of cuts and bruises. Her supervisor, in response to inquiries about what had happened, related this story. Two weeks earlier a teenage girl was brought to the hospital violently insane. She was the victim of a home where the word "love" was never heard, to say nothing of its ever being felt. No one ever told her that she was wanted. She felt nothing but rejection. She knew nothing but poverty, hatred, and violence. Her parents were alcoholics. She experienced the trauma of seeing her father fall to the floor dead from a gunshot wound inflicted by her mother. Although the mother was charged with manslaughter she was paroled, ostensibly to care for the little girl. The life style of the home continued without change. Beatings and cursings from her mother were common. The mind of the little girl, so filled with resentment and hate, finally snapped. The attending physician recommended that her therapy include allowing her to vent her wrath on someone and spew out some of the hatred that had poisoned her. The physician called for a volunteer, and this young nurse responded. Every day for two weeks she allowed her patient to vent her hate and resentment. She was kicked, scratched, and clawed until, in exhaustion, the child would slump into a corner, her body trembling like a frightened, trapped animal. After this painful ordeal the nurse would leave the cell. She would pause at the door and face the little girl, smiling through the blood that stained her face, and repeat these words. "Darling, I love you. Darling, I love you." This is Calvary love.

ALL THINGS ACT HARMONIOUSLY

God works "all things together" so that they are in harmony with each other. There are three important aspects of this harmony.

First, there is DIVERSITY in the harmony. The beauty of an anthem is dependent on its various parts. Harmony in music is produced by diversity. So it is with life. Every event in life is under the authority of God, who has the power to harmonize experiences in a way that brings peace and pleasure to mankind, the crown and glory of His creation. He takes the discordant tone of sorrow and harmonizes it with the pleasing tone of joy and produces a blessing that enriches our life. The most exciting people I have met have been those into whose life God has woven the thread of sorrow and hardship. These ingredients have added luster and beauty to their life.

> My life is but a weaving between my God and me,
> I cannot choose the colors He worketh willingly;
> Sometimes He uses sorrow, and I in foolish pride
> Forget He sees the upper, and I the lower side;
> The dark threads are as needful in the weaver's
>   skillful hand
> As the threads of gold and silver in the pattern
>   He's planned;
> Not until the loom is silent and the shuttles cease
>   to fly
> Will God unroll the canvas and show the
>   reason why.

Second, we need to see the DESIGNER of the harmony. Who is capable of taking the bad and the good, the sickness and the health, the diversity and the prosperity, and blending them together and producing from them a beautiful life? Only God can do that. We trust Him, knowing that He loves us and that He knows how every experience fits into His master plan. He can take the greatest tragedy and work it out to our good.

In 2 Kings, chapter 4, is an interesting story of a young man in the school of the prophets who, by mistake, prepared pottage from poison gourds. The students cried to Elisha, *"O, thou man of God, there is death in the pot"* (vs. 41). But God empowered Elisha to "heal" the noxious pottage, and they could eat it without harm. So, God has the power to make the best of a bad mess. The touch of His hand can restore harmony to any discordant life and give it worth.

'Twas battered and scarred, and the auctioneer
  Thought it scarcely worth his while
  To waste much time on the old violin,
  But held it up with a smile.
"What am I bidden, good folks," he cried,
"Who will start bidding for me?
  A dollar, a dollar"—Then, "Two! Only two?
  Two dollars, and who'll make it three?
  Three dollars once; three dollars, twice;
  Going for three—" But no,
  From the room, far back, a gray-haired man
  Came forward and picked up the bow;
  Then wiping the dust from the old violin,
  And tightening the loose strings,
  He played a melody pure and sweet
  As sweet as a caroling angel sings.

The music ceased, and the auctioneer,
With a voice that was quiet and low,
Said, "What am I bidden for the old violin?"
And he held it up with the bow.
"A thousand dollars, and who'll make it two?
Two thousand! And who'll make it three?
Three thousand, once; three thousand, twice;
And going, and gone!" said he.
The people cheered, but some of them cried,
"We do not quite understand
What changed its worth?" Swift came the reply:
"The touch of the master's hand."

And many a man with life out of tune,
And battered and scattered with sin,
Is auctioned cheap to the thoughtless crowd,
Much like the old violin.
A "mess of pottage," a glass of wine,
A game—and he travels on.
He's "going" once, and "going" twice,
He's "going" and "almost gone."
But the Master comes, and the foolish crowd
Never can quite understand
The worth of a soul, and the change
    that's wrought
By the touch of the Master's hand.

Finally we find DELIGHT in the harmony. These
are difficult days in which we live, but a Christian
can experience delight in them. No phenomenon of
nature, fire, flood, storm, pestilence, famine, cold,

or any other thing can destroy the delight that comes in knowing that *"all things work together for good to them that love God... ."* The delight comes through seeing God turn each crisis into a blessing.

It is sheer delight to stand back and watch God take something that the devil conjured up for our destruction and change it for our good.

ALL THINGS ACT ADVANTAGEOUSLY

All things work together harmoniously for our personal good. We should first understand what is meant by "our good." It does not necessarily mean our joy. It does not even mean our happiness. Paul is referring to our spiritual development. Many things that happen to us do not bring joy, but that is not their purpose. Their purpose is that we might *"through suffering come into the measure of the stature of the fullness of Christ"* (Ephesians 4:13).

God takes the evil that comes to us and transforms it into benefits that cannot be measured. The evil done to Joseph at the hands of his brothers resulted in immeasurable blessing. Joseph said to his brothers upon their arrival in Egypt for grain,

Now therefore be not grieved nor angry at yourselves, that ye sold me hither: for God did send me before you to preserve life. For these two years hath the famine been in the land: and yet there are five years, in the which there shall neither be earning nor harvest. And God sent me before you to preserve you a posterity in the earth, and to save your lives by a great deliverance. So now it was not you that sent me hither, but God: and

*he hath made me a father to Pharaoh, and lord of all
his house, and a ruler throughout all the land of Egypt*
(Genesis 45:5-8).

He continued to describe the measure of the blessing in Genesis 50:20: *"But as for you, ye thought evil
against me; but God meant it unto good, to bring to pass,
as it is this day, to save much people alive."*

The examples of God turning sighing into singing by turning bad into good are endless. You are
no exception to God's loving care; and He will do
the same for you.

ALL THINGS ACT SPECIFICALLY

The condition for all things working together for
good is an unfettered love for God. We cannot live
for the devil and defy God's authority over our lives,
and expect the fulfillment of this promise.

The promise is specifically to those that love God.
This love must be more than that which is verbally
expressed. It must be evident in our lives. We say
we love Him and then show it in the strangest ways.
Dr. Perry Webb used to tell the story of a woman
who took a revolver and shot her husband. Throw-
ing herself over his body she cried, "Oh, I loved him,
I loved him. I loved him so." Dr. Webb retorted,
"I would rather be loved less and live longer." We
must make certain our love is genuine.

May the Holy Spirit remove your blindness to the
purpose of God for you so that your sighing will
give way to singing.

Do you believe God when He says, *"all things*

work together for good"? Let me suggest a rewarding little exercise. Take the first clause of the verse, "And we know that...," then list every frustrating, discouraging, unpleasant experience in your life and conclude the list with the promise "work together for my good." Now pray the following prayer:

Forgive me Lord, I've prayed in vain that You
would spare me grief and pain,
But not my blinded eyes can see these things
were best for me.
Don't spare me trouble if it will bring me close
to Thee
Don't spare me heartaches, You bore a broken
heart for me.
Don't spare me loneliness, for I recall Gethsemane.
Don't spare me anything that You endured for me.
Don't spare me failure if this is what is best for me.
Don't spare me sickness if this will make me call
on Thee.
Don't spare me suffering for I recall Your agony.
Don't spare me anything that You endured for me.
Don't spare me but give me strength to
follow Thee.

By Audrey Mieir
Copyright 1959
Manna Music, Inc.,
Hollywood 28, Calif.

BLIND TO THE PROVISION OF GOD

Romans 15:13

The provision of God is that of a blessed life. Blindness to the availability of such a life always results in a life of sighing. This truth can be illustrated by an experience of my boyhood days. During my grade school years my father was pastor in the small southwest Missouri town of Humansville. At the edge of this little village was a clear flowing stream where three of my friends and I loved to swim. To add to the excitement, my friends tied a rope to a tree limb and would swing from an old root that extended out over the water. Their splash into the deep water gave them an extra thrill unafforded by my wading in the shallows. Not being the daring type, and a bit afraid of water, I lingered around the water's edge. This brought me no pleasure. While my friends were having fun I was enduring the outing. The happier they became, the more furious I became. One is seldom pleased to see everyone having a good time except himself. I finally decided to risk taking the plunge. I gripped the rope, swung out over the stream, lost my nerve, and found firm footing on the root of that old tree. I went home very disconcerted. The next day, determined to enjoy my swim to the fullest, I said, "Sink or swim, here I go." I will never forget the sheer joy that was mine as I took the plunge that day. From that day on, I was never satisfied lingering close to the bank in ankle-deep water.

The Christian life is much like that. Many people have accepted Christ as Savior but are lingering in the shallows, fearful to commit their lives completely to Him and take the plunge to enjoy the fullness of blessing. Just as I stood on the water's edge unhappy, while my friends were having a wonderful time, these defeated Christians stay where it's safe. There is no happiness in this kind of commitment. This life soon becomes one of sighing. One reason for the sighing that characterizes so many believers is that they are blind to the joy of the blessed life and do not enter into its fullness.

In Romans 15:13 the Apostle Paul outlined five aspects of this blessed life which if appropriated will change your sighing into singing.

THE SOURCE OF THE BLESSED LIFE

"Now the God of hope fill you with all joy and peace in believing, that ye may abound in hope, through the power of the Holy Ghost" (Romans 15:13).

Everyone is in search of a happy life, but unfortunately many are tapping the wrong source. Diamond Jim died leaving twelve million dollars without finding such a life. He fell in love with a woman named Lillian Russell. He gave her a check one day for a million dollars to be hers on the condition she would accept his proposal to become his wife. She tore the check into shreds, and Diamond Jim laid his head on the table and wept. "There ain't a livin' woman that would marry an ugly bird like me." The most important possessions in life cannot be bought. The blessed life is obtained not through self-effort but by going to the proper source and accepting it as a free gift. That source is God.

Paul knew the "God of hope." Are you without hope today? No wonder you are sighing. The moderator of a church business session opened the meeting by praying, "O thou eternal, most holy, most wise God in whom nothing is impossible"; on and on he prayed. At the close of the prayer he opened the business session by saying, "Now I think you will agree with me that our church has a problem to which there is no solution." How many times we engage in meaningless prayer to God for whom nothing is too hard and then complain that we have a crisis from which there is no escape. We whine and sigh in contradiction to our profession. There are no hopeless situations, only people who grow hopeless in them.

THE SATURATION OF THE BLESSED LIFE

Paul says the Blessed Life is filled to overflowing, which means it is saturated through and through with the Spirit of Christ. You are filled with something. Nature abhors a vacuum. I don't know what you are full of, but you are full of something. You may be full of self, anxiety, care, envy, resentment, anger, or some other sin that blights your life. If you want to know what you are full of, do this little experiment. Hold a glass of water in your hand and ask someone to bump your arm. Now, what spills out of the glass? Water, of course. The simple reason is that water was in the glass—whatever was in the glass spilled out. If you want to know what you are filled with, notice what spills out when you are bumped. Does the fruit of the spirit in Galatians 8:21-22 spill out, or is it some manifestation of self? The blessed life is one saturated with the very life of Christ, and His qualities rise to the surface at the slightest injury. Whether we sigh or sing at such injury depends upon what saturates us.

THE STRATEGY OF THE LIFE

The strategy of this life is seen in the word "believing." Are you having difficulty trusting God with your life? You trusted Him with your soul, didn't you? Is there anything more important than your soul's salvation? If He can be trusted with your eternal life, can He not also be trusted with your temporal life?

Jesus spoke to this problem of unbelief in the Sermon on the Mount. He warned against anxiety for temporal needs: *"Behold the fowls of the air: for they sow not, neither do they reap, nor gather into barns; yet your heavenly Father feedeth them. Are ye not much better than they?"* (Matthew 6:25,26).

How astonishing that just as I began to write

these particular words about the trust of the fowls of the air, the birds outside my motel room began to sing, confirming their carefree attitude toward life and their dependence on their Creator. They are singing beautifully this morning, and not because their barns are full of grain, for they have no barns. They neither reap nor sow, but the Father provides, and that is enough for them.

> Why should I feel discouraged, Why should the shadows come,
> Why should my heart be lonely And long for heav'n and home,
> When Jesus is my portion? My constant friend is He;
> His eye is on the sparrow, And I know He watches me.

> I sing because I'm happy, I sing because I'm free,
> For His eye is on the sparrow, and I know He watches me.

> "Let not your heart be troubled," His tender word I hear,
> And resting on His goodness, I lose my doubts and fears;
> Tho' by the path He leadeth, But one step I may see:
> His eye is on the sparrow, And I know He watches me.

Whenever I am tempted, Whenever clouds arise,
When song gives place to sighing, When hope
within me dies,
I draw the closer to Him, From care He sets
me free;
His eye is on the sparrow, and I know He cares
for me.

Would you like to live that kind of life? It is
attained by believing in God and His promises
to you.

THE SATISFACTION OF THE LIFE

The satisfaction of the life is expressed in the
word "abound." The blessed life is a satisfying
life—it abounds yet more and more. When Jacob
prohesied concerning the future of his sons, he said
of Joseph, *"Joseph is a fruitful bough, even a fruitful
bough by a well, whose branches run over the wall"*
(Genesis 49:22). Life in Christ abounds.

Speaking of the unceasing satisfaction He can
bring, Jesus said, *"...if any man thirst let him come
unto me and drink. He that believeth on me, as the
scripture hath said, out of his [innermost being] shall
flow rivers of living water"* (John 7:38). The phrase
"rivers of living water" speaks of an inexhaustible
supply. When I was pastor of the First Baptist
Church of Poplar Bluff, Missouri, my wife and
I frequently visited nearby Big Springs State
Park. Big Springs is the largest single spring in the
world, producing five hundred forty million gallons

of water every twenty-four hours. With delight I would lie on my stomach and drink from the refreshing stream, and the amount of water I consumed went unnoticed.

We often hear people say as they come from a spiritual service, "I got my cup filled today." Jesus is not engaged in filling cups. His method is collecting cups and substituting a river of living water. As Jesus rested by Jacob's well a woman came to draw water. Jesus said to this much married woman, *"Whosoever drinketh of this water shall thirst again: But whosoever drinketh of the water that I shall give him shall never thirst; but the water that I shall give him shall be in him a well of water springing up into everlasting life."* The woman replied, *"Sir, give me this water, that I thirst not, neither come hither to draw"* (John 4:13-15). *"The woman then left her waterpot and went her way..."* (vs. 28). She went rejoicing with a well springing up into everlasting life.

You see, Jesus collects waterpots and cups for very obvious reasons. If all you have is a cup you must continually come back for more. If you have a river of living water inside you in the person of the Holy Spirit, your satisfaction is inexhaustible. See what happens if you live by the cup philosophy. You get your cup filled on Sunday morning, and on the way home someone runs a red light, or the children fuss, and you grow irritable and spill your cup. This means you must continue all through the day with an empty cup until you come back to the church that night for a refilling. On the contrary, the river of living water gives immediate supply.

When Ishmael was born to Hagar, Abraham's handmaid, both mother and son were cast out by Abraham's wife, Sarah. Abraham gave Hagar a bottle of water and sent her into the wilderness of Beersheba. Soon the water in the bottle was spent, *"and she cast the child under one of the shrubs"* (Genesis 21:15). She was resigned to the worst, for she turned her back and said, *"Let me not see the death of the child."* She lifted up her voice and wept. The Lord, keenly aware of her plight, opened her eyes, and she saw a well of water (vs. 19). She arose and found refreshment. The empty bottle had left her destitute. Are you facing a desperate situation, and have, like Hagar, exhausted all your resources and your bottle is empty? Open your eyes to the *"well of water springing up into everlasting life."* This well will provide a blessed life of satisfaction that shall never run dry.

THE STRENGTH OF THE BLESSED LIFE

The strength of the blessed life is through the power of the Holy Spirit. We are without strength and incapable of accomplishing anything apart from the power of the Holy Spirit.

A famous heart surgeon was lecturing in one of our universities on the subject of heart transplants. The lecture was concluded by a question and answer period. One student asked, "Doctor, have you ever saved a life?" The noted physician replied calmly, "Yes. One." Then he related this story.

"One afternoon," he said, "I was called to a home in the country where a man was dying. I stayed with him most of the night. The patient was not responding. His wife asked if she could use a home remedy, and I told her the request would be granted if her husband showed no signs of improvement in thirty minutes. I asked her what the home remedy was, and she said it was to kill a goat and place the skin around the patient, and the warm body heat of the goat would draw out the infection. Fortunately, the man began to respond to the medicine, and the home remedy was not used. As the gray of the morning appeared, I went to my car to return home and saw a little goat in the corner of the fence. I said, 'Little goat, you ought to appreciate me. I saved your life.' Yes, young man, I have saved one life." The great heart transplant surgeon was acknowledging the powerlessness of his skill apart from the healing power of God.

You and I have not the strength to bear up under life's burdens, but a new dynamic is available to every believer, said Paul, "through the power of the Holy Spirit." With such a blessed life available to you, why sigh? Sing, brothers and sisters, sing!

BLIND TO THE DIAGNOSIS OF GOD

1 Corinthians 3:1

It would be enlightening if we could see ourselves as others see us. It would be more revealing still, if we could see ourselves as God sees us. The Bible says, *"God looks upon the heart"* (1 Samuel 16:7). When He looks upon the heart He gives His diagnosis. He makes it clear in His word what this diagnosis is, and elaborates on this pernicious ailment. What is this ailment that produces the painful and sorrowful sighs in the lives of so many Christians?

Scientists report that rich gas deposits deep beneath the earth's surface can be located by a certain kind of insect that is attracted by the volatile fumes. These insects leave their tracks and those tracks identify the pockets of gas. We as Christians leave tracks of good or evil that reveal the state of the soul deep beneath our exterior. God analyzes these tracks, and His diagnosis is that our condition is one of carnality. *"For ye are yet carnal"* (1 Corinthians 3:3).

Such carnality produces a life of sighing. The reason is very obvious. Carnality is a contradiction to our profession. We profess one thing and practice another. We believe but do not behave. We "talk the talk" but do not "walk the walk." The Chinese have a graphic way of describing such a contradictory life: "The head and heart do not agree." This, incidentally, is their description of a nervous breakdown. Distress always results when our head and heart do not agree. Paul described this dilemma in Romans 7:22, 23: *"For I delight in the law of God after the inward man: But I see another law in my members, warring against the law of my mind, and bringing me into captivity to the law of sin which is in my members."* We know in our head what is right and good, but with Paul we sigh, . . . *"but how to perform that which is good I find not"* (vs. 18). Giving mental assent to the principles of the Christ-life is one thing, but putting them into practice is another. Professing one thing and practicing another produces carnality, and carnality in turn produces sighing.

If you are in a state of sighing and desire the Lord to put a melody into your heart and a song upon your lips, get honest with yourself for the next few minutes and determine to open your eyes to God's analysis of your spiritual condition. The purpose of this chapter is to help you identify carnality in your life, that you may adequately deal with it so that the joy of your salvation may be restored. Singing and carnality are incompatible.

What are some of the tracks that will identify the presence of carnality in your life?

THE TRACK OF INCOMPETENCY

Incompetency means lacking in skill or ability. The carnal Christian lacks these qualities. He is incompetent. First, he is INCOMPETENT TO SERVE. Hebrews 5:12 reads, *"For when for the time ye ought to be teachers... ."* The writer rebuked these Christians of many years for their lack of knowledge which disqualified them from rendering a worthy service. Think of the number of people in our congregations who have been Christians for years but whose carnality has thwarted their spiritual growth, robbing them of the joy of service.

In my twenty-five years in the pastorate I have observed that the individuals who require the most pampering are the people who think only of themselves and refuse to reach out in ministry to others. Real joy, whether in the marriage relationship or other interpersonal relationships, is derived not from being served but from serving. Too many of us live in a little world of mirrors, and everywhere we look we see ourselves. We need to break away from these mirrors, enabling us to see the needs of other people and reach out in ministry to them. It is impossible to be used as an instrument of God to bring health and healing to a human being and at the same time live a sour and sighing life. No Christian is genuinely happy until he or she is ministering to others.

The fresh waters of the Sea of Galilee are alive with fish and other creatures but in the waters of the Dead Sea there is no life. The difference lies in the nature of the two seas. The Sea of Galilee gives in rich abundance as it flows into the Jordan; the Dead Sea, the recipient of the flow, keeps all it receives. There is no outlet—its death lies in its selfishness. The two seas and their characteristics symbolize the liberal and selfish lives and their nature. The Christian who is altruistic in nature and is always giving of himself is full of life. We can conclude that one cause for sighing is incompetency in service.

Sighing is caused not only by incompetence in service, but also by INCOMPETENCE IN COMPREHENSION . "...ye have need that one teach you again" (Hebrews 5:12). The emphasis in on the word "again." They had been taught before, but because of their carnality they could not comprehend spiritual truth. The inspired writer, in verse 11, describes this failure to comprehend, "Of whom we have many things to say, and hard to be uttered, seeing ye are dull of hearing." Spiritual truth cannot be comprehended by spiritually dead people. Dead people cannot eat or drink.

A frequent complaint I hear from patients I have visited in the hospital is loss of appetite. The most delicious dishes are unappealing, a sure sign that something is wrong physically. One thing I have noticed about such loss of appetite is that it is not accompanied by joy. Without question one of the reasons for the sighing Christian is his loss of appetite for the Word. Hebrews 6:5 speaks of tasting "the good word of God." The Psalmist said, "Thy commandments are my delights" (Psalm 119:143). If the Word of God brings delight it is logical to conclude that the absence of delight reveals a failure to feed upon the Word. It is impossible to taste the good word of God daily without being delivered from a life of sighing defeat to one of singing victory.

THE TRACK OF INCAPABILITY

The incapability of the carnal Christian is seen in 1 Corinthians 3:2. Paul said that the carnal Christian is incapable of eating strong meat. He can neither eat it nor digest it. He has no hunger to go deeper into the Word.

A diet without solid foods will not provide adequate nourishment. Lack of proper nutrients makes one irritable and fussy. The immature Christian who chokes on the meat of the Word is true to his infantile nature and does a lot of crying and whining. Occasionally someone will hurt his feelings because, according to him, "The preacher was preaching right at me." The pastor in an effort to see his people grow into full maturity will increase the strength of the diet. It requires a degree of maturity on the part of the hearer to say, "The pastor's message is convicting me, but I know it is for my good." Incapability to digest the meat of the Word is a sure track that reveals carnality, which results in a loss of joy.

THE TRACK OF IRRECONCILABILITY

The problem of irreconcilability is revealed in 1 Corinthians 3:3-4, "...*for whereas there is among you envying, and strife, and divisions, are ye not carnal,*

*and walk as men? For while one saith, I am of Paul;
and another, I am of Apollos; are ye not yet carnal?"*

The barrier separating Christian believers from
their unwillingness to be reconciled is an unmistakable sign of carnality. Carnal Christians always
have difficulty in interpersonal relationships. No
Christian can be happy as long as a reconciliation is
not made. You can know where a person is in his
Christian life and how he relates to the person of
Christ by observing how he relates to other Christians. John said, *"If we walk in the light as He is
in the light, we have fellowship one with another:"*
(1 John 1:7). If by walking in the light we have
fellowship one with another, an impaired fellowship indicates that we are walking in darkness.

Few factors in the Christian life are more responsible for sighing than broken relationships which
are irreconcilable. Is there some person with whom
you need to be reconciled? Have you been unable to
forgive the person of some wrong? You cannot live
victoriously with an unforgiving spirit. Failure to
forgive will destroy you. You must remember that
it is not the actions of people who destroy you; it
is your reaction to their actions. This is what Jesus
meant, I think, in the story of the mote and the
beam. It imagines a humorous scene of a man with
a beam protruding from his eye, while saying to
another, "I see you have a splinter in your eye, and
if you will hold still for just a moment, I will do
you a favor and remove it" (Matthew 7:3-5). The
mote represents the fault we see in the other person,

the beam of our reaction to it. The proportionate size of the mote and the beam reveals that our reaction is more grievous to the Spirit than is his action.

How then are we going to respond to the actions of people who threaten our peace of mind? There is a solution. Two doctors, a general practitioner and a psychiatrist, went up on the same elevator each morning. The general practitioner would get off on the ninth floor, and the psychiatrist would continue to his office on the twelfth. Each morning when the first doctor stepped off the elevator he would turn and spit on the other. After days of observing this procedure the elevator operator inquired, "Doctor, why does that man always do that to you?" The psychiatrist, taking a handkerchief and drying his face replied, "I don't know. That's his problem."

The actions of other people are not our problems. If we could only live dead to ourselves and alive to the needs of other people we would discover that their actions reveal a deeper problem, and they are crying out for help. How tragic it is that our usual response is to sever relations with such people. This response proves unredemptive to them and destructive for us. Estrangement from our fellow man results in estrangement from God. Estrangement from God results in Loss of Joy.

THE TRACK OF INSTABILITY
Paul speaks of this aspect of carnality in Ephesians 4:14, *"That we henceforth be no more chil-*

dren, tossed to and fro, and carried about with every wind of doctrine.... ". We can never be happy with unpredictable behavior. A capricious life characterized by uncontrolled changes is never a pleasant one. We must find the stability that comes from a sure and steadfast anchor.

I remember that when I was in college a chapel speaker told of a fisherman who, when retiring for the night, tied his boat to the trunk of a tree. During the night heavy rains came and the river flooded; his boat was sunk, leaving nothing but the chain in sight the next morning. A few yards away the fisherman saw a boat intact that had survived the same storm. He asked the owner why his boat was spared while his own was destroyed. The man replied, "You anchored your boat too low to the trunk of the tree, and when the waters rose the pull of the boat was down. If you'll notice, I anchored mine high, and the boat rose with the tide." The pull of the boat was up. The storms of life will assail the boat of your life and you will be tossed to and fro unless you firmly anchor to Jesus Christ.

Instability is the seedbed of a sighing life. You have never seen anyone sing who was tossed about by every change in his life. It is a sure cause of sighing.

> Will your anchor hold in the storms of life,
> When the clouds unfold their wings of strife?
> When the strong tides lift, and the cables strain,
> Will your anchor drift, or firm remain?

We have an anchor that keeps the soul
Steadfast and sure while the billows roll,
Fastened to the Rock which cannot move,
Grounded firm and deep in the Savior's love.

It is safely moored, 'twill the storm withstand,
For 'tis well secured by the Savior's hand;
Though the tempest rage and the wild
   winds blow,
Not an angry wave shall our bark o'erflow.

When our eyes behold through the gathering
   night
The city of gold, our harbor bright,
We shall anchor fast by the heavenly shore,
With the storms all past forevermore.

PART III

THE RELEASE FROM SIGHING

THROUGH PORTRAYING THE BEAUTY OF GOD

Exodus 34:29

We move now from the "reasons for sighing" to the happy and welcome subject of "release from sighing." This is what we all want. Bless God, this is what we all can achieve. The release is yours to enjoy. No one need live in utter defeat. In this chapter, by portraying the beauty of the Lord, we will see how one is released from sighing to singing.

This truth is beautifully set forth in an experience in the life of Moses, recorded in Exodus 34:29, *"And it came to pass, when Moses came down from mount Sinai with the two tables of testimony in Moses' hand, when he came down from the mount, that Moses wist not that the skin of his face shone while he talked with him."*

Moses had spent forty days and nights in the mountain alone with God. Being alone with God meant that he looked upon no other. Often we become like those to whom we devote ourselves. It is no wonder, then, that Moses came down from the mountain with his face aglow, reflecting the beauty of the Lord whose face he saw. A beautiful corollary to this account is 2 Corinthians 3:13-18. Verse 18 is of special significance: *"But we all with open face beholding as in a glass the glory of the Lord, are changed into the same image from glory to glory...."*

Think of it, "change from glory to glory." This means that we are transformed from one degree of glory to another. What a contrast from one degree of sighing to another!

The brightness that shone on Moses' face was a reflection of the effulgence of God's face. Spend time seeking God's face; since our face is a mirror, we will reflect God if He is in our line of sight. If your face is furrowed by sighing, it is evident that it is not our Lord you are reflecting.

The release from sighing and the vanishing of the harried look does not come through self-effort, but through being close enough to God to reflect His beauty. Paul said that when we behold the glory of the Lord we are changed. Notice two aspects of this change which all of us want to see effected in our lives.

THE CHARACTER OF THE CHANGE

One basic characteristic of the change is its unmistakable evidence. The Bible says of Moses, *"the skin of his face shone."* Some people try to counterfeit this change by developing a look that denotes piety. Jack Taylor says it's an expression somewhere between a migraine headache and acid indigestion. False piety is detected easily, and no one is fooled but the pretender. While some counterfeit the change by developing an ostentatious, holy countenance, others parrot the vocabulary which they pick up from genuinely holy saints of God. It is easy to use the terminology without the life to support it. It is not so much what we say that gives evidence that we are being changed into His likeness; the real attestation is a transformed life.

> Not only by the words you say, not only by your
>   deeds confessed;
> But in a most unconscious way is Christ
>   expressed.
> It is a beatific smile, a holy light upon your brow?
> Oh, no, I felt His presence while you laughed
>   just now.
> For me 'twas not the truth you taught, for you so
>   clear, for me so dim;
> But when you came to me, you brought a sense
>   of Him.
> And from your eyes He beckons me, and from
>   your lips His love is shed,
> Until I lose sight of you and see the Christ instead.

Another important characteristic of the change is that it is not fully perceived by the one transformed. Scripture says, *"Moses wist not that the skin of his face shone"* (vs. 29). True Christian excellence is an unconscious of its beauty as was Moses. The man who thinks he has a shining face is a counterfeit. A woman is never charming who thinks she is. A man loses his handsomeness the moment he becomes aware of it. In a real sense, the less spirituality one has, the more he feels he has to impress. I have noticed when we try to imitate a person whose qualities we envy, we usually exaggerate. This tendency is also true in the spiritual life. When spiritual gifts and Christian qualities are imitated by people of lesser commitment, the result is that they usually overdo it. One of the great dangers of imitating the excellence of others is that we have not experienced the events in their lives which caused them to live in this way; this particular style may not be God's will for us.

A husband watched one day as his wife put a ham into a pan for baking. She did a strange thing that puzzled him. Prior to placing it in the pan she cut the end off the ham, which to him seemed unnecessary. When he asked the reason for this she replied that her mother always cut the end off a ham before baking it. Weeks later, while visiting his wife's parents, he said to his mother-in-law, "I want to ask you a question. Why do you always cut the end off a ham before you put it in the pan?" She replied, "That's the way my mother always did it." Soon after, the husband asked his wife's grandmother the same question. She informed him that she always cut the end off the ham because her pan was too small. Our imitation of other people's Christian qualities can be just as meaningless. We are to reflect Him, not what we see of Him in others. What we see in others may be only an imitation of the real thing.

The beauty of the Lord is not a mask we wear but a life we live. It is evidenced by the quiet inner confidence that enables us to bear up under pressure. I was privileged to be at the bedside of my pastor father during his last hours on this earth, and I saw this quality in him during those closing hours. One night he appeared to be dying; as the dawn broke, when he blinked his eyes, I bent low and asked, "Dad, do you want something?" With his innate humor unabated by the pain of dying, he replied, "No, I was just looking to see if I was still here."

THE CERTAINTY OF THE CHANGE

To behold the glory of the Lord and be changed into that same image from glory unto glory is a change that we can experience for certain. The privilege of transformation from sighing to singing through portraying the beauty of the Lord is not limited to a select few. Would you like to have a shining face? You can certainly have it. There are some principles we must follow that were evident in Moses' transformation.

First, WE MUST DARE TO BE OPEN. 2 Corinthians 3:18 reads: "...*with open face beholding as in a glass the glory of the Lord.*" Just as the canvas must be toned to a neutral tint on which the artist paints his masterpiece, our lives must be open and un-prejudiced to allow the reflection of the Lord to come through unblemished. We must present to God a yielded heart.

In ancient days a shining face was a sign of beauty. Today that is not true. Women today attempt to prevent their faces from shining by the use of cosmetics. We will never see the significance of the relationship of the oil to the shining face unless we know the source of the oil. Oil comes from the crushing of the olives, symbolic of the crushing and heart-breaking experiences of life. The shining face comes as a result of the pressing. The Greek word THILIPSIS describes this painful procedure. It conveys the idea of pressing together. The application of this word to human suffering was used in the New Testament. The first-century Christians thought of themselves as being in the vat, like grapes or olives, and being pressed to the point where their joy ran out like wine or oil. Is it possible to press joy from sorrow as one presses wine from grapes or oil from olives? Oil and wine are Biblical symbols of joy. Oil was used as a cosmetic to make the face shine. Thus, it became a symbol of joy and singing. *"The Lord bless thee and keep thee, the Lord make his face to shine upon thee... "* (Numbers 6:24-25).

The Lord has made it clear He wants us to be men and women with shining faces, reflecting joy and gladness. Nevertheless, many of God's children have fallen short of God's best and are living a life of sighing. There is a release from this sighing, but it is a painful one. Olives and grapes are fruits that produce oil and shine, but they are not oil and wine in themselves. Some olives and grapes are never used for oil and wine. They remain on the vine or tree until they become hard and pulpy dry. Such olives and grapes are better than nothing, but they are not substitutes for oil and wine.

If you are satisfied with only olives and grapes, they will dry up in your storehouse. Symbolically oil and wine bring joy and singing, but olives and grapes do not. You must see that it is impossible to have the oil and wine unless the olives are crushed and grapes pressed. The believer who experiences pain and suffering for Christ's sake will produce the oil and wine that make the face shine and the heart rejoice. Dear old F. B. Meyer used to say, "The traveller who would pass from the wintry slopes of Switzerland into the summer beauty of the plains of Italy must be prepared to tunnel the Alps. The Garden, the Cross, and the Grave are the only way to Easter morning." It seems indispensable that we should pass into the shadow of bereavement, temptation, and distress if we are to emerge into God's marvelous light.

Not first the light, and after that the dark,
But first the dark, and after that the light.
First, the thick cloud, and then the rainbow's arch;
First, the dark grave, and then the resurrection
    light.

Another imperative to reflecting the beauty of the Lord is A WILLINGNESS TO BE ALONE WITH HIM. *"Be ready in the morning and present thyself there to me in the top of the mount, And no man shall come up with thee"* (Exodus 34:2). This time alone with God can be achieved by the development of a quiet time at the beginning of every day. I would commend to you Dr. Stephen Olford's booklet *Manna in the Morning* as a guide to such an exercise. There is no hope for deliverance from sighing to singing apart from a habitual and systematic quiet time.

> I met God in the morning when my day was at
>   its best.
> His presence came like sunrise, like a glory in
>   my breast;
> All day long His presence lingered, all day long
>   He stayed with me;
> And we sailed in perfect calmness o'er a very
>   troubled sea.
> Other ships were blown and beaten, other ships
>   were sore distressed;
> But the wind that seemed to drive them brought
>   to me a peace and rest.
> Now I think I know the secret, learned from
>   many a troubled way,
> You must meet Him in the morning if you want
>   Him through the day.

THROUGH PARTICIPATING IN THE PRAISE OF GOD

Psalm 103:1

Many people are in mental hospitals today because they chose to pout instead of praise. It seems that human beings have an insatiable desire to find fault, criticize, and murmur. It is the nature of the "old man" to grumble. On the contrary, the person who has been made alive has a new nature; he is no longer bound by the desires of the flesh. The new nature wants to praise God and give Him thanks. We must remain close to God, however, or the old nature will again cause us to lapse into defeated sighing.

All of us at some time or other experience what the oldtimers used to call "the dark night of the soul." In these times we find release not from offering petitions to God but from offering praise. Who Jesus is, is infinitely more important than what He has to give. One of the reasons for our sighing is that we are seeking God's hands and not His face.

Nothing so completely turns our sighing into singing as praise to God. Triumphant singing always results when we sing in spite of it all. With his back bleeding and his feet in stocks, Paul in the Philippian jail sang at midnight (Acts 16:25-40). Revival broke out because he and his companion, Silas, chose to praise instead of pout. We must not wait until the trials are over to praise God. We praise Him when things are difficult. The prophet Habakkuk is a stirring example of this truth:

Although the fig tree shall not blossom, neither shall fruit be in the vines, the labour of the olive shall fail, and the fields shall yield no meat; the flock shall be cut off from the fold, and there shall be no herd in the stalls. Yet I will rejoice in the Lord, I will joy in the God of my salvation. The Lord God is my strength, and He will make my feet like hinds' feet, and he will make me to walk upon mine high places. To the chief singer on my stringed instruments (Habakkuk 3:17-19).

Job said, *"Though He slay me, yet will I serve Him"* (Job 13:15). David said, *"As long as I live I will praise the Lord"* (Psalm 52:9; 61:8). He called upon the sun, moon, and stars to praise Him. Mountains, fruit trees, cedars, beasts, old men, and children he exhorted to praise the Lord. He was determined that no catastrophe, no adversity, no trial would dissuade him from praising the Lord.

The key that releases us from sighing is praise. Four aspects of praise are seen in Psalm 103:1: *"Bless the Lord, O my soul, and all that is within me bless His holy name."*

THE PRACTICE OF PRAISE

David practiced praising the Lord. The Lord blessing us is a concept easily understood. But our blessing Him is incomprehensible. Our failure to understand fully the scope of praise must not prevent us from practicing it.

We can bless God through CONTINUAL CONTEMPLATION. This involves reflecting on who God is another way, we praise Him by thinking well of Him. Have your thoughts of God always been thoughts of praise? Have the turbulent and chaotic circumstances in your life caused you to think ill of God? The declaration of Job is a good one for us all: *"Though He slay me, yet will I trust in Him"* (Job 13:15). Your life may be experiencing unexpected hardships, but that must not prevent you from thinking well of God. The practice of praise should continue unabated despite the contrary nature of your circumstances.

We are to bless the Lord, not only through continual contemplation, but through PERSONAL CONSECRATION. This principle is seen in Christ's model prayer: *"Hallowed by thy Name, thy kingdom come"* (Matthew 6:9-13; Luke 11:13). Thy kingdom come refers to the bringing to earth of the quality and nature of the heavenly life. Astronauts live in space in a capsule called a "life-support system." In this capsule, which becomes their home in space, they are taking with them some of the earth's atmosphere. Living the Christian life is a reversal of this procedure. The Christian lives in the "lethal" atmosphere of earth by bringing to this planet the atmosphere of heaven. He is bringing to earth the kingdom of heaven. We can sit in heavenly places in the here and now (Ephesians 2:6).

Such heavenly existence requires personal consecration. Just as continual contemplation means "thinking well of Christ," personal consecration suggests "wishing well for Him." Have you ever thought of wishing Him well? This is what is implied in praying "thy kingdom come." Through personal consecration we live an exemplary life; and everywhere we go, the influence of the kingdom of God is felt. If we are living in a heavenly atmosphere, our very presence in a room results in the abating of hatred, the disappearance of ill will, and the dispelling of darkness. When we step into that room filled with people who are struggling in life's atmosphere, for that moment at least, the kingdom of God comes to that room. A Philadelphia paper carried a terse weather report one day which read, "It was a gloomy day in Philadelphia until Phillips Brooks came to town." Through personal consecration we not only dispel the gloom from our lives, but also from the lives of others.

Another way to praise Him is by our CONSISTENT CONVERSATION. If contemplation is "thinking well of Him," and personal consecration is "wishing well for Him" then a consistent conversation involves "speaking well of Him." If you want to bless the Lord, continue speaking well of Him. Few things are as abhorrent to me as listening to someone use the name of the Lord in vain. Christians sometimes speak His name with such frivolity, it borders on profanity. It could be, however, that a worse transgression is in not using His name at all.

In a worship service in a Congregational church in Keswick, England, I heard Dr. Stephen Olford give the greatest exposition of the 1st Psalm I have ever heard. The first part of the Psalm expresses the characteristics of a godly man. Dr. Olford said that the man of God opposes godless thinking; *"...walketh not in the counsel of the ungodly."* He opposes lawless living; *"...nor standeth in the way of sinners."* He opposes careless speaking, *"...nor sitteth in the seat of the scornful."* Dr. Olford made a poignant evaluation when he said that anytime you hear a person speaking carelessly, you may be sure he has come through every stage, beginning with "godless thinking," "lawless living," through to "careless speaking." This marvelous insight has its counterpart in what I have just said about "thinking well," "wishing well," and "speaking well" of God. When you hear someone speaking well of God you can know that he, too, has run the course from thinking well of Him and wishing well for Him. It all begins with the thought life. When people listen to your conversation they will know what you have been thinking.

THE PASSION OF PRAISE

The passion of praise is suggested as the text unfolds, *"Praise the Lord O my soul, and all that is within me...."*

David speaks first of spiritual praise: *"O my soul."* There is prevalent today a method of praise more sensual than spiritual. The last decade has seen the infiltration of music that borders on religious rock, and the sounds filling the sanctuary have not been very different from those spilling out on the streets from the nightclubs. The beat is the same; the only difference is that the lyrics have a religious connotation. Much of our music and "praise" is designed for entertainment instead of worship. Any program of "worship" designed to entertain rather than exalt Christ and edify His Body is sensual. Our preaching, praying, and singing should represent a praise that is spiritual.

Our praise should be not only spiritual but strenuous. David exclaims *"all that is within me."* Our worship service will be shorn of its power if all that is within us is not involved in praise. Many times only our body is involved in worship. Our mind is home in the kitchen, concerned about the burning of the roast, or on the golf course, or on our plans for the afternoon.

Almost everything else we do is done strenuously and energetically except praising and serving the Lord. The problem is that our efforts are mis-directed. Early in our marriage, my wife, who is fond of ice cream, wanted to buy an electric ice cream freezer. Pastoring a very small village church, I felt we could not afford such a luxury item. Confident of my inventiveness, I assured my wife that with my engineering skill I could, with little expense, create an electric freezer by converting the old one. I first cut off the handle with a hacksaw. That was my first mistake. I then constructed a large wooden pulley and attached it to the shaft, replacing the crank. The next step was to remove the motor from our washing machine. That was my second mistake. I was reminded of the farmer, milking his cow. The cow kept swishing her tail in his face, and he tied it to his leg. He said, "I hadn't been around the barn seven times till I discovered I had done the wrong thing." I had no sooner dismantled my wife's washer than I knew I had done the wrong thing. I worked industriously all through the day, and toward evening the freezer was ready for action. And there WAS action. When I plugged it into the current, parts flew all over the yard. It was a disaster. My problem was not laziness; I worked assiduously. My problem was that I misdirected my efforts. Wouldn't it be wonderful if we were as energetic in our praise as we are in matters of lesser worth? Our real problem in Christian circles today is that we are misdirecting our efforts and investing our energies in second-rate matters.

THE PURPOSE OF PRAISE

David expressed the purpose of praise: *"Bless the Lord...bless his holy name."* The purpose of praise is to make Him the supreme object of our adoration. Our Lord is to be the singular object of praise. The name "Lord" signifies that there is only one object of praise. The problem is not that we do not praise—all of us have an object of praise. It may be our companion, our family, our profession, or even ourselves. There is only one who is worthy of praise, however, and He is the Lord God.

We are to see our Lord as a sacred object of

praise: *"Praise His holy name."* Perhaps the greatest reason for the dearth of praise in our ranks today is our failure to respond to the holiness of God with a holy offering. Paul spoke of this kind of offering in Romans 12:1, *"I beseech you, therefore, brethren, by the mercies of God that ye present your bodies a lving sacrifice, holy, acceptable unto God which is your reasonable service."*

Do you attempt to substitute gifts of money and deeds of service and other lesser offerings for a holy life? There will be incomplete fulfillment in our walk so long as we fail to recognize that a holy God requires no less than the praise of a holy life.

THE PERSON OF PRAISE

David did not say, "Preacher, bless the Lord." He did not say, "Deacon, bless the Lord." He personalized it: *"Bless the Lord, O MY soul."* David was saying that he was not responsible for the practice of anyone else, but as for himself, he would praise the Lord. We must all engage in personal praise of our God.

First, personal praise is EDIFYING. The word "edifying" means to build up. Praise builds up. How do you behave when you are discouraged and downcast? Do you retreat and draw yourself into a shell and give up? The intelligent response to discouragement is to burst forth in praise. A Christian recognizes that victory has already been secured, and he praises God before it is actually seen. We are to praise God for victory in advance. The children of Israel marched around Jericho and blew their trumpets, claiming victory before the walls actually fell. You will remember, also, that they did not wait for the River Jordan to divide before they attempted to cross it to enter Canaan. God divided the waters and provided a dry river bed AFTER they claimed victory over the obstacle. If you are facing an obstacle of some kind, the Lord will build you up, and you will be personally edified if you begin now to praise Him for what He will do. If you are in the wilderness today, remember "...*he brought* [*you*] *out...that he might bring* [*you*] *in*" (Deuteronomy 6:23).

Of the giants of Canaan Joshua and Caleb said, "...*they are bread for us...their defence is departed from them, and the Lord is with us: fear them not*"(Numbers 14:9). To look upon the enemy as bread is certainly an edifying thing. Bread gives nourishment. The thought of being built up and edified by your enemies should encourage you to continually praise God.

Personal praise, second, is ENERGIZING. If you are chronically fatigued, what you need, perhaps, more than vitamins is to get yourself off your hands and feel the energizing sensation of praising the Lord. Many people are tired because they are expending their energy in worry and anxiety. When the energy is not wasted one can face indefatigably every crisis of the day. The person who sighs his way through life has not "entered into rest." The "rest of God" is not rest from labor, but rest in labor. An interesting insight into rest comes from the Old Testament. The priests were not allowed to wear woolen garments. Wool is hot and makes one sweat. One of the tragedies of the Christian community is that we are tired out from self-effort to such degree that our energy is dissipated and we have none left with which to praise the Lord. While most of us are left exhausted from self-initiated activity, we can find exhilaration and renewed strength through praising Him.

In the third place, personal praise is ENTERPRISING. The enterprising aspect of praise consists of thinking of praise as an adventure. The Christian life is the most adventurous life in the world. It is exciting to face every trial with curiosity, wondering how God is going to reveal His perfect will in and through the ordeal.

Let me remind you again, you will not pray your way out of a spiritual muddle. You will not read your way out of a spiritual muddle. If you have settled into a life style of sighing and you want to sing again, you must begin right now, at this moment, to praise. Praise the Lord whether you feel like it or not!

THROUGH PERFORMING IN THE FASHION OF GOD

Romans 12:17-21

Most children exposed to church life have included in their little fantasy games the playing of church. This was a favorite pastime of our youngest daughter, Patty. One day she and her mother were in the bedroom absorbed in a "pretend" church service when her brother, returning from school, opened the door and peeked in. Fearing this would break the spirit of the service, I suppose, Patty stood up and rudely slammed the door in his face, yelling indignantly, "You can't come in here; we're having fellowship!" I have always said she was not "playing" church as much as she thought. More than we would like to admit, that kind of reaction is prevalent among the average body of believers.

We have been thinking about the problem of the believer's sighing and how to turn it into singing. Such a study would not be complete without acknowledging that one basic cause for sighing is broken relationships and the failure to respond to them in a way that is pleasing to God. There is a way to react as well as a way not to react. Is there a person who has slighted or injured you in some way? Are there those with whom you have lost fellowship? You cannot ignore this problem and live a joyful and fulfilling life. Do you really want to be free from the bondage of a deteriorating relationship with that friend? Would you like to experience a restoration of that relationship, that the song might return to your heart again? Open your Bible to Romans 12:17-21 and notice how Paul treated this problem and how we can be released from the sighing it produces. As we shall see, the release comes through our responding in a way that is pleasing to God. In this passage Paul dealt with five truths which we must apply to ourselves if we want to experience such release.

THE PROHIBITION OF RETALIATION

"Recompense to no man evil for evil. Provide things honest in the sight of all men" (Romans 12:17).

The word "recompense" means "retaliate," to "pay back." Paul said we are not to pay back evil for evil. Retaliation in the Christian walk is prohibited. An effective TV commercial shows a State Trooper standing beside his patrol car saying, "You have been told that driving 55 miles an hour saves gasoline. You have also been told that driving 55 miles an hour saves lives. What you have not been told is that driving 55 miles an hour is the law."

You have been told that returning good for evil is best. You have been told returning good for evil is right. What you need to be told is that returning good for evil is the law. Paying back evil for evil results in your own destruction. Our only source of outside entertainment as children was an old Philco radio, with such a low volume, we all had to gather close around to hear the sound. My favorite program was Amos and Andy. Andy was irritated by a friend who had the habit of slapping him across the chest when they met on the street. One day Andy said to Amos, "This man is not going to do that one more time. I have a stick of dynamite in my vest pocket, and the next time he strikes me across the chest he's going to get his hand blown off." The irony is apparent: we cannot recompense evil for evil without inflicting personal injury.

We destroy not only ourselves through recompensing evil for evil, but also the individual who is the target of our retaliation. We must be sensitive enough to recognize that when a person does something to hurt us, this is his other way of saying, "I need help." If we know this, we will respond in love in an effort to build him up. Members of the body are to edify one another. I have seen such loving reaction operative recently in our fellowship. It is personally rewarding to respond in a way that is pleasing to God.

A PROVISION OF RIGHTEOUSNESS

The restoration of fellowship is closely associated with what I will call "a provision of righteousness." According to Paul, we must be honest. He was not referring to what we would call gross immoral acts so much as infractions in the "gray" area. Miss Bertha Smith of China has been a guest in our home many times. During a conference years ago she needed the counsel of a tax consultant, and a member of our church of that profession came to our home to confer with her. A particular item was being discussed, and Miss Bertha asked, "Is it legal?" The tax consultant replied, "Well, Miss Bertha, it's a bit questionable. It may be accepted as valid, but it is in the gray area." Without a moment's hesitation she quickly retorted, "I will not do anything in the gray area. I might want to pray sometime." Those of us who knew her are aware that hers is a life of prayer, and she did not want her prayers to be hindered by not providing things honest in the sight of all men.

The failure to provide things honest in the sight of all men breaks the relationship with God and in turn jeopardizes our relationship with others. I boarded a plane in Los Angeles recently and requested a seat in the nonsmoking section. Just two seats behind me was the No Smoking sign. A passenger desiring to smoke moved the sign closer to the front so he could indulge legitimately. His dishonesty in moving the sign to accommodate his own inclination was an infringement upon others who desired a flight free of smoke inhalation. Our failure to provide things honest in the sight of all men always inflicts some kind of injury to others that is a hindrance to an amicable relationship.

THE PROMOTION OF RECONCILIATION

"If it be possible, as much as lieth in you, live peaceably with all men" (12:18).

We are enjoined to promote reconciliation. It is our responsibility to live peaceably with everyone, if at all possible. Paul made allowances here. He said, *"If it be possible as much as lieth in you, live peaceably with all men."* There are some people with whom you cannot be reconciled. They will refuse to respond to any attempt you make to repair a breach. Still others do not get over one offense until their feelings are hurt again. The friendship is so fragile that it is a full time job simply keeping it in a good state of repair. When you have done everything you know, including the application of Matthew 18, and still there is no reconciliation, rest the case with the Lord.

THE PREVENTION OF RETRIBUTION

"Dearly beloved, avenge not yourselves, but, rather give place unto wrath; for it is written, Vengeance is mine; I will repay, saith the Lord" (12:19).

Paul says "avenge not." The word "avenge" means retribution—getting even with someone. It is our nature to balance the scales, to "get even," to avenge. My wife, standing in the yard one day, was astonished to see our son Phillip, five years of age, punch a little neighbor boy in the nose, knocking him to the ground, whereupon the little boy sprang to his feet to return the blow. Phillip, using scripture to his advantage, said, "Be ye kind one to another." The neighbor reacted naturally in desiring to seek vengeance, and my son did the natural thing by resenting it. The supernatural is required in altercations like this. The supernatural is available when we take seriously the words

"Vengeance is mine; I will repay, saith the Lord." We must leave vengeance to the Lord.

Abraham deceived Abimelech when he told him Sarah was his sister but failed to mention that she was also his wife. When Abimelech discovered this deception he said to Sarah, *"Behold, I have given thy brother a thousand pieces of silver: behold, he is to thee a covering of the eyes, unto all that are with thee, and with all other: thus she was reproved"* (Genesis 20:16). The statement "he is to be a covering of the eyes" means "I have defended you in the presence of your friends." God will always defend His own. God will always make right the record. One of the most meaningful verses that substantiates this truth is Deuteronomy 32:35. God said, *"To me belongeth vengeance, and recompence; their foot shall slide in due time: for the day of their calamity is at hand, and the things that shall come upon them make haste."* The Lord is assuring us that if we retreat from the fray, put up our swords, and let Him fight the battle, the events bringing about the destruction of the enemy will surely come. God says, "Their foot will slip in due time."

As a general rule, the destruction of an enemy is his own doing. Left to his own devices be brings calamity on his head. The story is told of a blacksmith who was captured by an invading army and imprisoned. He was tied to a ball and chain. He knew that every chain had one weak link, and when night came he could identify the faulty link simply by a touch. When the weak link was identified he could break it and escape. That night as he felt of the chain he identified it as one made by his own hands. His chains had no weak links. He knew there would be no chance of escape—he was a victim of his own handiwork. One of the most tragic sentences in the Bible and human existence is Esther 7:10, *"So they hanged Haman on the gallows that he had prepared for Mordecai."* Haman was not the only man who has suffered calamity at his own hands. God says, "I will repay," and this seems to be the method He uses.

THE PENETRATION OF THE REACTIONISTS

"Therefore, if thine enemy hunger feed him; if he thirst, give him drink; for in so doing thou shalt heap coals of fire on his head. Be not overcome of evil, but overcome evil with good" (Romans 12:20,21).

I am calling this section the penetration of the reactionist because defiant, quarrelsome, resistant people can be penetrated if the correct principles are applied. Paul says we can reach them by heaping coals of fire on their heads. This is accomplished by feeding them when they are hungry, and giving them drink when thirsty.

Years ago ore was melted by placing a fire beneath and charcoal above. Fire on the head of an antagonist is caused by our willingness to overcome evil with good. Two options are open to us with respect to our attitude toward evil, according to Paul. We can be overcome by it, or we can overcome it.

The Christian should be one who demonstrates to the world that disputes between believers can be resolved. If believers cannot find release from a life of sighing to one of singing, who can? Why don't you this very moment turn your gloom to His glory and go on through life with this song ringing in your heart?

Thou hast changed my gloom to glory
   Joy in Christ I've found;
Sin renounced is sin forgiven,
   I'm no longer bound.

Like the bread on yonder hillside,
   When the crowd He fed;
He has broken my proud spirit,
   Now by Him I'm led.

From the darkness of the midnight,
   Thou hast brought me through;
By thy grace and tender mercy,
   I've found life anew.

All to Jesus I have given,
   Every attitude;
My rebellious sinful nature,
   Christ my Lord subdued.

Love is flowing like a river,
  Deep from in my breast;
Since the day I came to Jesus,
  And received His rest.

Come to Jesus for the cleansing,
  Of that gnawing sin;
He will hear the vilest sinner,
  And invite him in.

John B. Wright